Insanely Effective Network and Multi-Level Marketing for Introverts on Social Media

Learn How to Build an MLM Business to Success by the Top Leaders in the Field and Why You NEED to Start RIGHT NOW!

By Ray Schreiter & Tom Higdon

Table of Contents

Insanely Effective Network and Multi-Level Marketing for Introverts on Social Media

Table of Contents

Introduction

Chapter 1: What You Need to Know About Network Marketing and Multi-Level Marketing (MLM)

>What Is the Difference Between Network Marketing and MLM?
>Should I Start Network Marketing or Build My Own Business from Scratch?
>What Benefits Do I Gain from Network Marketing Companies?

Chapter 2: Master Your Mindset Above All Else

>Envision Your Dreamy End Goal
>Spend 10 Minutes A Day Dreaming
>List 3 Things You Want to Achieve and Achieve Them
>Give Yourself a Pep Talk
>Hold Yourself Accountable
>Pay Attention to Your Thoughts
>Build an Inspiring Team of People
>Stay Curious

Chapter 3: Choosing The Right Company for You

>Choose Your Niche and Discover Companies
>Consider the Stability and Longevity of the Company
>Evaluate the Products and Services
>Learn About the Compensation Plan
>Pay Attention to The Specific Team You're Joining

Determine If the Business Fits with Your Goals
Making The Final Pick of Which Company You Choose

Chapter 4: Making A Commitment to Growth

Learn to See the Good in Things
Commit to Working Hard Toward Success
Continue Approaching Growth with Consistency and Passion
Respect Yourself and Your Needs
Focus On Expanding in Every Way That You Can
Be Willing to Seek and Accept Feedback from Others
Commit to Learning About Your Business and Industry

Chapter 5: Promoting Your Products and Events

Build A Brand for Yourself
Take Advantage of Video Marketing
Create Content Specifically for Your Ideal Client
Attend Events That Your Audience Would Attend
Show the Products in Use
Don't Focus Entirely on Sales

Chapter 6: Presenting Your Opportunity to Prospects

Invite Them to Approach You
Let Them Ask the Questions
Lead The Conversation without Pressure
Subtly Create a Sense of Urgency
Have a Resource Available for Them to Read Over
Always Request to Follow Up

Chapter 7: Converting Prospects into Distributors or Customers

Spend Time Getting to Know Your Pitch

Initiate the Conversation with a Question
Answer Any Questions Your Prospect Might Have
Make Your Pitch

Chapter 8: Creating A Strong Follow-Up System

When to Use Automated Follow-ups
When to Use Manual Follow-ups
How to Create an Automated Follow-up System
How to Create a Manual Follow-up System
Knowing When to Stop Following Up

Chapter 9: Building an Effective Downline

Finding Prospects for Your Downline
Engaging with Your Prospective Downline
Qualifying Your Downline to Find the Best Team Members
The Importance of Service-Based Leadership
'Be A Leader, Not a Boss
Learn How to Manage Your Time
Stay Consistent in Your Leadership
Keep The Lines of Communication Open
Encourage Your Downline to Leverage Their Strengths
Train, Inspire, and Motivate

Chapter 11: Handling Rejection like a Pro

Detach from the Outcome Before You Even Start
Consider Asking Why They Rejected Your Offer
Refrain from Investing Your Emotions into It
Do Not Look at Rejection as a Means to an End
Handle Rejection with Poise, Grace, and Integrity
Make Sure You Respect Yourself

Chapter 12: Why Some People Don't Make Money?

They Don't Have Enough Focus
They Never Learned How to Market Properly

They Didn't Position Themselves as a Leader
They Didn't Target Their Niche Effectively
They Tried to Make Things Too Complicated
They Got Impatient
They Chose to Blame Others for Their Mistakes or Failures
They Never Actually Wanted to Succeed

Conclusion

Book Description

Introduction

Congratulations on downloading *Insanely Effective Network and Multi-Level Marketing for Introverts on Social Media*!

This book is the ultimate guide to help you understand how you can run a powerful network marketing or multi-level marketing business even if you are an introvert. Inside of these pages, you are going to learn everything you need to know to run a successful business that will earn you a great income and help you enjoy the life you truly aspire to live.

Network marketing companies and multi-level marketing (MLM) companies have had a highly controversial reputation in the past. Some people believe that they are incredible, and others believe that they are a scam. In this book, I am going to prove that they are not what people say they are and that you can definitely make a great amount of money through your network marketing company.

As soon as you learn these strategies and begin applying them into your business, you are going to discover that network marketing truly is not as hard as some people make it look. Furthermore, you do not have to resort to annoying and spammy marketing methods in order to make money with this business model. In fact, you do not want to be pushy or spammy at all. Instead, you want to focus on running a business that is going to have integrity and dignity. To do that, you may want to use what is known as "attraction marketing," which I will elaborate on in the succeeding chapters.

I am also going to show you how you can conduct a sales conversation, convert prospects into clients or distributors, and lead a team. Virtually everything you need to run a powerful network marketing business is outlined in this book. As long as you are willing to stay committed and put the work in, you can feel confident about generating the types of results that you want to create with your business.

If you want to get the maximum value out of this book, you need to be ready to put in the work. This book highlights the importance of knowing what to do and doing it properly. Everything you are going to learn is practical, effective, and guaranteed to help you attain the success you want in your MLM business.

It is important that you realize that in taking on this venture, you are taking personal responsibility for your business. You are responsible for your success and results, and it is up to you to put in the work needed to create them. If you want to experience massive success, you have to be dedicated to learning what it takes to generate massive success.

If you are ready to begin learning about how to have an incredible business that is going to help you generate maximum success and earn a great income, it's time to begin! Dive in to learn about what makes network marketing so great and how you can make work for you.

Chapter 1: What You Need to Know About Network Marketing and Multi-Level Marketing (MLM)

Network marketing and multi-level marketing (MLM) are two forms of businesses that are based on a peer-to-peer selling structure. Over the years, network marketing and MLM companies have gained a controversial reputation. Generally, those who take the time to learn how this structure works find themselves making a great deal of profit as opposed to those who don't. In fact, network marketing and MLM companies are known to have produced more millionaires than virtually any other industry to date.

There are many reasons why people join network marketing companies, but the biggest one is that it has the biggest potential to support you in reaching your income goals. Before I begin teaching you about how you can make a killing off of your network marketing business (even as an introvert), I want to show you what exactly you are getting into.

What Is the Difference Between Network Marketing and MLM?

Network marketing and MLM are both peer-to-peer selling structures, but they work in two unique ways. While network marketing is more based on direct sales, MLM focuses on building a team.

The network marketing structure is sometimes referred to as "direct sales" because the primary emphasis is on selling a product to consumers. Essentially, business is conducted through a middleman. The company that you are working for will sell you catalogues and other marketing materials, and then you go to your consumer and sell them the product. The consumer then purchases it, and the company compensates you for that sale.

In some cases, network marketing distributors choose to purchase some popular stocks to keep on hand so that they can get the product to the client faster. This increases appeal and supports the individual in generating more sales, but it is not necessary.

When it comes to starting a network marketing business, your primary focus is identifying potential customers in your network and selling them products. Because the market can be competitive, there are also many other ways to meet new people and add them to your list of prospects. I will show you exactly how to do that in this book!

MLM, on the other hand, is similar to network marketing, except that it involves including a team of distributors building underneath you. In network marketing, your primary focus was to sell products to potential customers. In MLM, however, you want to focus on selling to customers *and* recruiting other distributors. Based on the nature of the pay scale, you are encouraged to invite other people to become distributors underneath you. In doing so, you build what is called a team or a downline.

With MLM, you are paid in more ways than just selling to customers. You are also paid for your downline and everything they sell, too. So, in this case, you stand to make a lot more money if you are willing to put in the effort to have people join underneath you. In this book, I will also cover how you can build a team and how you can be a strong leader so that your team earns more money and, as a result, so do you.

Should I Start Network Marketing or Build My Own Business from Scratch?

Before you launch into any new business venture, you always want to make sure that you are making the right choice. In this case, you might be wondering if you should go with network marketing or MLM, or if you should just build your own business from scratch. While you are certainly welcome to do anything you desire, I want to make sure that you understand exactly what comes with either option.

When you choose to start a business from scratch, you are choosing to take on a lot of work. For people who know exactly what they want to do or are passionate about making products or services to sell, this can be a great option. However, they must also realize that this comes with a lot more responsibility, too. Launching your own business means that you are solely responsible for things, such as branding, marketing, creating products or services, selling, incorporating, handling legal fees and taxes, managing your online presence, and more. Depending on the nature of the company, you might have to work on supplier acquisition and finding stockists who will actually sell your products. Then, to top it off, you also have to shoulder all of the financial aspects related to starting the business. You could always consider a loan, but then you have to pay that money back plus interest. If you were to choose investors, you would have to factor in their thoughts and opinions, which could get messy.

On the other hand, network marketing and MLM are a lot simpler. You can still choose an industry and products or services that you are passionate about. Then, all you have to do is market the products to prospective clients. You are not responsible for finding and hiring manufacturers, storing products, shipping products to clients, managing websites, and the like. You simply purchase your marketing materials, market the products, and receive your commission for doing so. However, because you are an independent distributor, you are still classified as an entrepreneur, and you carry all of the great benefits of being one, i.e. setting your own schedule and having an unlimited earning potential.

What Benefits Do I Gain from Network Marketing Companies?

There are several benefits that you can gain from working with a network marketing or MLM company. Aside from setting your own schedule and having an unlimited earning potential, there are many other reasons why people love getting involved in these companies.

One major reason is that when you join a network marketing company, there is a smaller amount of risk that you incur. With your own company, you put a lot of your own money and assets on the line to start the business. When you are a distributor with an MLM company, however, the company itself takes on any liability. This means that if anyone has any complaints, money is lost, or time is wasted, it is lost by the company and not you. You still receive your check, either way, as long as you have sold your products and services.

Another benefit you stand to gain is that you are marketing products that are already tested and known for high quality. When you are starting your own business, testing products and finding high-quality ones can be costly and time-consuming. When you start with an MLM company, this process has already been done. Anytime a new product comes to the product line for you to market, it has already undergone testing and experiments to make sure that it is high quality. As a result, you can always be confident in the quality of the products that you are marketing to your audience.

When you choose to go with a network marketing or MLM company, you have the unique opportunity of generating what is known as a "residual income." Residual income is, essentially, income that you gain but do not have to trade a direct amount of hours in exchange for a set amount of money. In other words, once you have your downline established and customers who are regularly purchasing products, your money will continue coming in. While you will still want to focus on growth, a certain amount of your income will already be practically guaranteed every month. This means that you can focus on spending time doing things that you love rather than trading your time for a paycheck.

If you are the type of person who loves the idea of a freedom-based lifestyle where you can do anything you want, go anywhere you want, and do it all whenever you want, MLM and network marketing are a wonderful solution for you. These companies are generally based online in the modern world—meaning you can do virtually anything you want and go anywhere you want without worrying about your business. Instead, you can easily take trips, go on vacations, move around, or live the nomad lifestyle all while making more cash.

There are clearly many reasons why network marketing is a powerful business model when done right. As long as you follow the strategies I give you in this book, there is no reason why you cannot be another one of the millionaires earning their income through independent sales.

Chapter 2: Master Your Mindset Above All Else

Before you can achieve anything, you need to focus on mastering the mindset associated with the success of your venture. When it comes to a business venture like network marketing or MLM sales, you are going to find that there are many people with many different opinions. Sometimes, those opinions are not optimistic. In fact, some of them can be the exact opposite. If you do not spend time getting crystal clear with your own mindset and energy, you are going to find yourself struggling to stay optimistic in your business. If you have a hard time staying optimistic and excited, your customers and team will struggle, too. Then, your business will most likely fail.

I suggest starting with mindset first because it can ensure that you are mentally prepared for any challenges that you may face starting from day one. This does not mean that it will be a challenge right off the bat, but as with anything, there will be a learning curve. Ensuring that you are mentally prepared to withstand this learning curve and generate success will keep you on track to earn a great deal of money in your business in the long run.

The strategies that I am going to give you in this chapter are ones that you need to start exercising right away. Some of these strategies are going to be ones that you need to be doing on a daily basis. Others are ones that you can reserve for when you are having a hard time in your business and need an extra boost of optimism to keep you going. Having these in your toolkit now and practicing them from day one will strengthen the impact that these tools have on you. As a result, they will work exactly as you need them to when it comes to helping you achieve the success that you desire from your business.

Envision Your Dreamy End Goal

The first thing you need to do before starting your MLM business is to dream about what you want it all to look like. Spend some time really engaging in the dream and deciding everything that you want to have. In order to do this productively and effectively, make sure that you are dreaming as if there are no limitations on what you can do, as there really aren't any. If money, time, and resources were not an issue, what exactly would you want to be doing with your business—with your life? Get deep and insightful with this vision, and be as specific as you can.

If you want, you can create a vision board for this. Find pictures, words, articles, and anything else you desire that reflects what is in your dream. Then, keep the vision board handy so that you can see it at least once per day. This is a wonderful way to motivate yourself and stay focused.

Spend 10 Minutes A Day Dreaming

As you work on building your business, commit to spending 10 minutes every single day to dreaming. Spend this time dreaming about what you want the end result to be like, what it will feel like, and how you are going to enjoy it. You can do this in any way you want. You might spend that ten minutes dreaming about what the perfect day would look like, looking at a highlight reel of all of your best achievements, or simply enjoying the dream of doing one thing that you long to do when you achieve your success.

Research suggests that spending just ten minutes every day dreaming about your desires supports you in manifesting them. During this ten minutes, you mentally prepare yourself for the lifestyle and demands that will be placed upon you from having the success that you desire. This is a great way to overcome feelings of worthlessness, to prepare yourself for the changes, and to mentally understand what will be required in order for you to get there. When you imagine yourself doing it, the process of actually getting there and believing that it is possible is not so hard.

List 3 Things You Want to Achieve and Achieve Them

Every single day, you can work toward conditioning yourself for success and discipline by setting a goal to accomplish three things. Then, make sure that you actually accomplish them. These three things should, in one way or another, be tied in with your success, even if they include taking a nap so that you can be more rested for running your business.

By setting small goals daily, you set yourself up for success by conditioning your mind to want to achieve your goals. Each time you achieve these smaller goals, your mind feels a rush of endorphins like serotonin that reward it for the accomplishment. As a result, you become far more excited by success, and it is easier for you to continue working toward larger goals. Plus, these smaller goals are the necessary steps toward actually reaching your larger goals. It is a win-win situation!

Give Yourself a Pep Talk

During times that you are struggling in your business, refrain from bullying yourself or getting caught up in self-doubt and pessimism. It can be easy to feel as though ruts are forever or somehow permanent, but they're not. Each time you find yourself feeling as though you are in a rut or noticing the energy of self-doubt creeping in, set the intention to give yourself a pep talk. As soon as you notice it, start.

Pep talks do not have to be hard or elaborate. Simply reminding yourself of your dream and reminding yourself that you have what it takes is enough. You might consider recalling times that you faced adversity and overcame it with strength and success, or even reminding yourself as to the many reasons why you wanted to start your business in the first place. Staying focused on the end goal is the best way to continue giving yourself pep talks as needed so that you can experience greater success in your business. Pep talks can be a part of your daily routine, or they can be reserved for those moments when you are feeling as though the route to success is more of a struggle than you had anticipated it would be.

Hold Yourself Accountable

When it comes to generating success on any level, you have to be willing to hold yourself accountable. When you make a commitment, be the kind of person who is willing to do whatever it takes to see that commitment come through. It can be challenging at times, but it is essential. Not only will fulfilling the commitment bring you one step closer to achieving success, but it will also help you prove to yourself that you are capable of doing so.

Anytime you make a commitment to do something— whether it is to yourself, to your downline, or to your customers— be impeccable with your word. Do not go back on your commitment, and do not hold back from achieving success. Make sure you do everything you can to stay true to your word. If, for some reason, you absolutely cannot, make sure that you come up with a viable solution or alternative to help you, your downline or your customer achieve their goals. Your commitment and your devotion are necessary: no one else is going to do this for you. Start from day one, and you will be mentally dressed for success.

Pay Attention to Your Thoughts

Your thoughts have the capacity to build you up or tear you down. They can do the same for your business, too. If you are not staying disciplined with your thoughts, you might find yourself mentally sabotaging your success. You need to trust that you have what it takes to succeed and consciously dim down the inner voice that keeps telling you that you can't. Anytime you notice it coming up and telling you that you are incapable, unworthy, or unable to succeed, begin affirming to yourself that you are capable, worthy, and able of creating success.

Be willing to notice these thoughts and take control. Consciously choose to think thoughts that are going to help move you toward success, rather than take you away from it. When you put the effort into thinking positive thoughts, your ability to stay optimistic is significantly improved. This means that it will be easier for you to stay focused and generate the success you want because your own inner pessimism will not be sabotaging your results.

Build an Inspiring Team of People

Sometimes, nothing is more helpful than an empowering and inspiring system of support helping you succeed. In MLM businesses, you have a unique opportunity to build a team of people who are all working toward the same goals on one level or another. As a result, you can selectively choose to build your team in a way that supports success right from the very beginning.

When you are building your team of downlines, focus on using the advice I give you in this book to develop a strong community of people. Through this, you can create a culture of positivity, optimism, support, and inspiration. As a result, all of you will have a powerful team to fall back on any time you are feeling discouraged or doubtful with your business. This support network is unparalleled in how it will help you and your entire team continually work toward success.

Stay Curious

The power of curiosity is magnificent. When you are curious, you search for answers. You can use this curiosity as a way to magnify success in your business and keep you moving forward. Stay curious about what lies in store for you. Stay curious about where a little bit more effort or the next level can do for you. Stay curious about what you can achieve. Stay curious about everything. The more curious you are, the more wonders you will be filled with. This energy keeps you looking and moving forward.

Replace your fear with curiosity. Replace your doubt with curiosity. Replace your discouragement with curiosity. Replace anything holding you back mentally with a sense of curiosity. Wonder what you can do, and then seek to find the answers by moving forward and staying committed and focused. When you do this, success becomes much easier because you are curious about just how much you can achieve, rather than worried that you may not achieve any at all.

Chapter 3: Choosing The Right Company for You

Now that you are equipped with a powerful mindset that is ready to succeed, it is time to equip yourself with a company that can get you there! Choosing the right company is essential. Once you choose your company, you need to stay committed. This is how you are going to maintain your branding, keep your image intact, become known as the "go-to" person for that product or service, and climb the ranks. Each time you restart with a new company, you have to rebrand yourself, get the word out there, and rebuild your downline. Rather than having to put in the work multiple times, it is better just to commit and do it all once! To be able to do so requires that you have the right company to support you along the way.

In this chapter, I am going to show you exactly what you need to consider and how you can find the right company for you. You are going to discover what matters, what is required in order for you to achieve success in your business, and how you can discover if a company is going to be a perfect fit for your long-term when it comes to achieving your goals. I must stress the importance of making sure that the company you desire to join fits *all* of the criteria. Do not join a company just because your good friend did, or you might end up with a company that will not serve you long-term. Look at the following criteria, and think critically before starting. Remember: this is a business move, and it needs to be treated like one.

Choose Your Niche and Discover Companies

Before you can evaluate a company for whether or not it is worth your time, you need to consider what companies you want to evaluate! This requires you to identify what niche you want to be a part of and what companies exist within that niche. There are a few ways that you can do this, but ultimately, it comes with finding a niche that you are passionate about, that is profitable, and that has a strong MLM company in it that you can join. Without these three factors, the company might not be worth your while.

To determine what niche you want to be in, consider your top two or three interests that you feel could be profitable. There are many out there, such as health and beauty, fashion, finances, career, and more. Consider what ones are the most interesting and important to you and start there.

After you have determined which your top two or three are, I want you to evaluate them in terms of how profitable they are going to be. You need to pick a niche that is going to have the capacity to earn you a great deal of money. If you pick one that is too small or not growing, you will quickly realize how hard it is and that you may not actually be able to make a profit in that niche. You want to do some online research to discover the size of the niche, who the target audience is, how much money it earns, and whether or not it is growing. If it is growing and has a strong audience size, chances are it is a great place for you to get into.

Lastly, do another search to find out which companies are in your desired niche. This shouldn't be too hard; simply type in "(chosen niche) MLM companies in (your country)." This will bring up a list of all of the different niches available to you in your country that fall under your niche. I suggest writing all of these names down and doing research on all of them to make sure that you don't overlook a potentially great candidate.

Consider the Stability and Longevity of the Company

When you are looking into the companies that you have identified, there are some critical pieces of information that you need to pay attention to. In particular, you need to focus on determining how strong the company is, how stable it is, and how long it is likely to be in business for. Some companies are in business for decades and continue to grow with great strength. Others die off after only a couple of years. It is important that you pick one that is going to last and stay stable so that you can continue making an income for a long time.

It is important that you realize that if the company does go under, you will lose everything with them. You want to pick one that is going to stay around for a long time and that will continue giving you the opportunity to earn a greater income. You can learn about this through a few different points of information.

The first thing that you need to consider is how well-capitalized the company is. You want one that has plenty of capital to grow, that is continuing to focus on growth by launching new products and services or opportunities, and that has a clean track record for paying people their commissions. One that seems to have very little extra capital or that struggles to grow or pay its distributors is one that you should avoid, as these are companies that are beginning to show signs of potential failure.

Another thing that you need to consider is how old the company is. Companies that are less than five years do offer ground-floor opportunities and, if you have a good eye for such things, could be a great opportunity. After all, if you are one of the earliest distributors, you are more likely to grow people under you. However, if you are a ground-floor distributor on a company that does not succeed, this doesn't mean much. If you are not entirely sure about how to evaluate the longevity of a business *idea*, which is an entirely different book altogether, you are better off choosing a company that has been around for at least five years. This shows that the company is out of the startup phase and has reached a degree of stability that should keep it around for many years to come.

Evaluate the Products and Services

In addition to evaluating the company itself, you need to evaluate the products that they are selling, too. You want to make sure that you are choosing to sell for a company that has unique products. If their products are too similar to something that you can buy in store or elsewhere, chances are your audience will flock to that option instead because it's simply easier and faster than waiting for the shipment to come in. However, if your product is unique, your audience will understand why it is worth the wait and will have nowhere else to go to avoid shipping times.

You also have to make sure that the products being sold by the company are desirable. The last thing you want to do is find yourself trying to sell products that people truly do not want. Your product needs to provide tremendous value to the customer if it is going to be able to sell, so pay attention to this. In addition, make sure that your unique and desirable product is priced right. The last thing you want to do is find yourself trying to market something that is priced higher than the average customer is willing to spend. The only people who will purchase things at these higher prices are other distributors so that they can reach their compensation plan goals, which can put you in a difficult position when it comes to selling products and growing your business.

Lastly, make sure that the product you are choosing is not just the result of a trend or a fad. Choosing something that is likely to be irrelevant or obsolete in a few months' or years' time can result in you putting a lot of work into building your business only for it to fall flat when people move on to the next trend. While businesses that incorporate trends into their products to maximize sales are genius, businesses who build their entire company based off of a trend are not. The former knows how to expertly use trends to boost sales, whereas the latter does not have a strong plan for future growth, meaning that there likely won't be any. You do not want to be stuck with your wheels spinning on a business that loses its marketability in a few months or years. Instead, you want one with products that will continue to serve your audience for a long time to come.

Learn About the Compensation Plan

Since you are getting into this business to get paid, it is essential that you pay attention to the compensation plan. Choosing a company with a poor compensation plan is going to result in you struggling to earn a strong enough profit. In fact, you may even find yourself earning virtually nothing at all. There is nothing more tragic than hearing stories of people who have put tons of effort and attention into their businesses and climbed the rankings only to be several levels up in the company and still earning just a couple hundred bucks a month.

You need to choose a company that is going to help you start earning a lot as soon as possible. This comes from picking a company that has a great compensation plan. There is no fixed framework for what constitutes a great compensation plan. As long as you don't find yourself putting in tons of work and being paid pennies for it, the plan should be considered a good one.

However, as you go about comparing companies to determine which ones are the best, you should compare compensation plans, too. That way, you can choose the company with the best plan that meets the other criteria and fits your needs.

Also, pay attention to bonuses. Most companies offer bonuses if you hit certain goals or if you achieve certain achievements. While these do not necessarily have to be the deciding factor for you, knowing what you can expect to earn on top of your regular commissions can be nice. Choosing companies that love to offer bonuses regularly and that offer many other prizes or rewards for reaching certain targets can be nice. Typically, these companies are more considerate of their distributors and will offer better incentives to work your business. This can mean plenty of wonderful bonuses and added benefits for doing the same amount of work!

Pay Attention to The Specific Team You're Joining

Aside from the company itself, pay attention to the team that you are considering joining under. The company and products are both essential to your success, but so is a strong team. Starting a new network marketing company without a strong team can result in you not having the inspiration, motivation, and support when you need it. Alternatively, it can result in you feeling outcast if the team is too cliquey and does not make room for new team members. Unfortunately, this can happen, and it can be a big discouragement when it comes to running your business.

Ideally, your team and the person introducing you to the opportunity should be committed to helping you succeed. You should feel confident that they are going to be just as committed before you join as they will be after, too. Finding a team that is filled with strong leaders who are committed to helping each other succeed ensures that you are going to have all of the resources that you need to succeed. In addition, it will show you how you can best lead your own team so that you can stay committed to their success, too.

A good way to discover more about your potential team is to ask about who the team is, how it is led, what types of activities are involved, and what the support is like. You want a team and a leader who are going to train you for success, not just ones who are going to recruit you, collect a check, and abandon you to move on to their next recruit. If your sponsor will let you, consider asking for a chance to take a "sneak peek" at what the team is like by inviting you to a training call or event. This is a great way to get an inside-view at how the team works together and if they will be able to support you and your future team in creating success going forward.

Determine If the Business Fits with Your Goals

Remember the dream you dreamed up in the last chapter? Here is a great way for you to begin calling upon that dream to start serving you right now. Consider that dream, and consider each business and how it would fit into your dream. Does it have the offers that you want? Is the opportunity the right fit? Does it make sense? If you find a company that serves you with everything you need to make your dream come true, chances are you have found a great company.

You always want to make sure that your MLM company fits into your life, not the other way around. You should not feel like you are trying to adjust your life to fit the needs of the business. After all, this is what you are likely trying to get away from when leaving your job. Learning how to fit your business into your life properly can take time and practice, as you have to learn how to let go of your employee mentality and let your company factor you in, not the other way around. However, once you learn how to view your opportunity from the eyes of a boss, it becomes a lot easier to see how the company is going to fit into your lifestyle and support you in creating your dream life.

If the company does not have the potential to fulfill your dream life alongside you, chances are it may not be the right one for you. Even if it is a great company with great earning potential and profitability, you do not want to pick a company at the expense of your happiness. You need something that you can be passionate about and that will bring you joy. Believe me—if you pick a company that you are not passionate about, people are going to be able to tell, and growing your company will be a lot more challenging. Your passion is infectious, so you are likely to grow much faster with a company you are genuinely passionate about than one that you are not, even if the opportunity seems better on paper.

Making The Final Pick of Which Company You Choose

Once you have put all of your consideration in towards your choice, it is time to choose! Choosing at this point should be simple, but I want to make sure that you feel confident in making your choice. So, to recap: you want a company that will be around for a long time with great products that customers want and are willing to pay for. You also want to make sure that their compensation plan is strong enough to earn you a great profit, that it will help you grow quickly, and that it will not take too long or be too challenging to begin earning that profit. The team you are considering to join needs to be inspiring and supportive and willing to train you so that you can achieve your desired success. You also need to have a genuine passion for the company and products that you will be selling, as you do not want to find yourself in a company that you do not enjoy. If you are unsure about whether or not you are passionate about the company and their products, consider starting out as a customer first. Then, if you do feel that you are passionate enough to sell them, you can consider them as a potential business opportunity.

If your ideal business meets all of the above criteria, chances are it is a great business to start with. This is everything you need to create a strong opportunity to build a massive business that is going to help you get rich and earn residual income, so it is essential that you are a stickler about having these criteria met. If even one of these areas is weak, you might risk your ability to earn enough money to make your dreams come true. It absolutely must be the right fit for you if you are going to succeed.

Chapter 4: Making A Commitment to Growth

If you want to have a successful business, you need to have growth. A business without growth is just a failure. You do not want your business to fail, so you need to commit to growth. This is how you are going to ensure that your business succeeds and that you earn the income that you desire through your business.

When it comes to committing to growth in favor of your business, there are two areas that you need to commit to— personal growth and professional growth. Both of these areas of growth are going to support you in achieving the magnitude of growth required to experience success.

Personal growth is going to support you in growing in a way that supports your success. Personal growth contributes to your ability to mentally handle the growth that you are facing, to see the good in everything, and to stay positive and in an optimal state of mind to achieve your growth. If you let yourself stop growing, it will be a challenge to grow your business because you will not have the commitment or drive that you need to continue climbing the rankings to success.

Professional growth is important, as this is going to teach you how you can do better at your business. You want to know how you can become a better leader, a better seller, and a better marketer. You want to pay attention to opportunities to discover how you can learn more about your product and industry so that you become a great resource for your downline and customers. Also, you want to make sure that you can understand what it takes to grow and put in the work required to do so.

When you commit to your personal and professional growth and put an honest effort into both, achieving success becomes inevitable. That is because you are ensuring that you have all of the resources and knowledge required to make success happen. I have outlined below how you can begin achieving personal and professional growth right now so that you can grow your business to be a beautiful empire right off the bat.

Learn to See the Good in Things

Learning how to see the good in everything is a wonderful way to begin discovering opportunities everywhere. Realistically, everything is an opportunity for growth or success. All you need to do is know how to see the opportunity and take advantage of it to put it to work for you. If you want to achieve growth and excellence, you need to learn how you can see the good in things around you so that your eyes stay open and that your mind stays optimistic.

In addition to helping you see opportunities that you can take advantage of, learning to see the good in things is going to help you train your downline to do the same. As a result, you will end up having a strong team of individuals who are committed to growth and excellence, too. This will support all of you in seeing opportunities and continually working toward growth so that each of you continues to experience great success in their businesses.

Commit to Working Hard Toward Success

Hard work pays off. While your business will not always be hard, staying committed and focused is essential, and being willing to put in the work is the only way to achieve success. When you are working, focus on spending the least amount of time doing the most productive tasks possible. This will ensure that your time is spent working hard and achieving results that translate to growth. It will also keep you from wasting any time or spinning your wheels trying to achieve more growth while doing things that are not really getting you anywhere. The people who have the most time are the ones who use theirs wisely.

Hard work does not necessarily require you to be doing back-breaking labor or putting yourself through the ringer every single day just to see growth. Instead, focus on doing things that push you out of your comfort zone and force you to take the next steps toward the next level. Put effort into getting out of your head and into your plan so that you can take the necessary action to create the growth that you desire. Then, do it again. Keep doing it until you achieve success.

Continue Approaching Growth with Consistency and Passion

The more you stay consistent and passionate about what you are doing, the easier it is going to be for you to continue growing. Without consistency, your passion has nowhere to be applied. Without passion, your consistent effort lacks soul and purpose. You want to keep everything focused and working toward your goals with a strong level of passion and drive.

Consistency and passion are going to do two things for your business: they will keep you in the right frame of mind to grow, and they will keep your audience paying attention to you. Because you are setting the pace for yourself, continuing to put in the effort required to achieve success is a lot easier. You become used to it, and your commitment to growing your business becomes an enjoyable routine that you look forward to every single day.

In addition, because your audience sees you staying passionate and continually talking about your opportunity and products, they become curious. When people realize that you are serious about what you are doing and that you are committed to making growth happen in your business, they focus on you more. They realize that there is probably a reason as to why you are still passionate about your business, and they grow curious about what it is and why you have not given up yet. Hence, they are more likely to want to try it out. If you stay committed and passionate, your team and customers will, too.

Respect Yourself and Your Needs

When it comes to growth, committing to understanding yourself better and having a greater sense of self-awareness is important. Understanding yourself and your needs and respecting yourself enough to advocate for yourself ensures that you always feel as though you are working in satisfying or desirable conditions. This ensures that you are never feeling overworked, taken advantage of, or mistreated in your company or business.

People who do not advocate for themselves and practice self-respect for their needs find themselves feeling rundown and exhausted. As a result, their businesses suffer. They may not have the energy to keep up anymore, or they may even find themselves resenting their businesses and avoiding doing them. Since you own your business and you are the only person holding yourself accountable, if you let yourself feel rundown to the point where you do not want to work anymore, no one can stop you. As a result, you might end up giving up on the very business that could have brought you the success that you desire.

Rather than letting yourself get run down and resentful, pay attention to your needs, and make sure that they get fulfilled. If you feel that you have been working hard and that you need a break, schedule some time off. If you feel that you are giving a great deal to your team and not enough to yourself, let them know that you are taking some time off, or consider asking some of your more knowledgeable distributors to begin supporting you in training new team members. As you grow and as your needs change, always make sure that you are taking account for them and respecting yourself in the process. The more you take care of yourself and feel good about doing your business, the easier it is going to be for you to generate growth in your company.

Focus On Expanding in Every Way That You Can

A commitment to growth means a commitment to expansion. You need to be committed to expanding in every way possible: from learning more about yourself and how you work best to discovering more about your company and how you can grow even bigger. The more you commit to expansion, the easier it is going to be for you to identify opportunities and grow. Then, once you see these opportunities, make sure that you also make a commitment to actually giving them a try.

While you may not want to put work into every single opportunity, and while you might find out that they will not bring you as much benefit as you have hoped along the way, the effort you put in will teach you a lot. As you learn to identify these opportunities, you will teach yourself to discover which ones are worth following and which ones might not be the best idea. Then, you can begin following the ones that are worth your while and applying all of your knowledge and skill into making them a success.

The more you recognize unique opportunities and commit to giving everything a try and learning as much as you can, the more you stand to learn. When the business owner becomes complacent and believes that they have already learned everything that they need to know, this is when they begin to lose out. This is especially true for business owners who rely on marketing as their primary source of income. Marketing is constantly changing, so committing to knowing more and doing more is the best way to ensure that you are going to learn everything you need to know to master the expansion in your industry.

Be Willing to Seek and Accept Feedback from Others

We can only see so much in the mirror and in our self-awareness and self-reflection. As humans, we simply cannot pick up on everything that we do and criticize it so that we can discover how to do better. While we can certainly learn a great deal, there will be things that we miss over or that we may not even realize that required growth or development.

Asking for feedback from those who work with you on a regular basis and taking it critically is a great way to begin discovering ways that you can grow more. When you spend time listening to what other people notice and giving them the opportunity to guide you, it allows you to have a spotlight shone on areas of yourself that you may not see otherwise. Feedback is a wonderful way to recognize new opportunities for how you can grow and do better in your life and in your business.

When you are listening to feedback, always make a conscious effort to refrain from getting judgmental or defensive when people offer it. It can be difficult to take feedback in a constructive way that supports you in actually learning more and doing better with what you learn. However, once you discover how much you can learn by listening and taking in the feedback that you are given, you will find that you can grow so much more when you are open-minded. Listen carefully to what people say, and think about it critically before discovering ways that you can apply the information to your growth. That way, you ensure that every adjustment you make and all the growth you work toward is actually supporting you in moving in the direction that you desire to go.

Lastly, when it comes to receiving feedback, always be cautious about who your feedback is coming from. While most feedback is well-meaning, you do not want to be taking too much feedback from people who do not understand your goals or who are unaware of what it takes to do what you desire to do. Taking feedback from people who are not actively educated on what it takes to do what you want to do might end up in you growing in the wrong direction or wasting your time on growth that is ineffective. Instead, try paying attention to those who you look up to and focus on learning more from them. These are the people who understand what you are doing more clearly and can offer you feedback that will actually help move you in the direction you want to go.

Commit to Learning About Your Business and Industry

No matter how long you are in your industry or business, you can guarantee that things are going to change. The more you commit to learning about your industry and staying educated on your business, the easier it is going to be for you to become a powerful resource to your downline and customers. Committing to becoming a knowledgeable resource means that people can count on you and come to you for advice and support when needed.

When people begin realizing that you know everything that they could possibly need to know about your business or industry, they begin to see you as an expert. Being seen as the expert means that people are going to trust that you are the one to go to when they need support. They will also point their friends and family in your direction because they know that you will have the answers they need. This results in greater exposure for yourself and your business—meaning a greater number of opportunities for growth and increased sales and recruitment volumes. It is well worth it to continue studying your business and industry so that you can become the expert and people come to you rather than searching for a different resource to help them.

Chapter 5: Promoting Your Products and Events

Having products and events where sales are involved is only worthwhile if you are actually going to promote them! As a network marketer or MLM distributor, your primary job is to promote your products and services and any events that you may have going on. This way, people know about you and what you are currently selling or where they can find you to get more products.

When it comes to MLM and network marketing it is essential that you promote effectively. Unfortunately, some people have a negative idea of what distributors are and how they market as a result of a few people in the industry who have had little to no training. However, you are going to learn how to market effectively, respectfully, with integrity, and in a way that actually *works*. In this chapter, I am going to show you the best updated strategies that are going to help you earn more customers and distributors using what is known as attraction marketing.

Build A Brand for Yourself

As a direct marketer, you are not bound to only the brand that is established by the company you are marketing for. In fact, if you want to be known as memorable and encourage people to purchase from you and not a different distributor, you do not want to focus solely on that brand at all. Instead, you want to focus on building a personal brand for yourself. Remember when I said that you want your business to fit into your life, not the other way around? This is a great opportunity to prove that this is the case.

When it comes to personal branding, you want to show your audience your entire lifestyle and how your company fits into it. This is going to achieve two things that support your business's growth. First, it will show your audience that you are a real person. People do not want to buy from someone who's entire page looks like an online catalogue. Instead, they want to buy from someone who has a personality and spends time bonding with their audience and building relationships with them. This has more meaning and feels better to your customer, helping them feel more interested in purchasing from you and feeling like they are personally appreciated for doing so.

Second, building a brand for yourself and showing off how your business fits into your life is a great way to show your audience how it could work for them, too. People who might be interested in starting a similar business will get to see how much fun you have and how the business becomes a part of your life. Because they also live a life, they will be able to relate to the life you are living. This allows them to begin thinking about how the company could potentially fit into their own life, too. As a result, half of the work is already done in getting them to join your team! All you have to do is give them the extra words of encouragement, and before you know it, you will have new members joining your team in no time.

Take Advantage of Video Marketing

Video marketing is growing in popularity. Even though you might be fearful of doing video marketing if you are an introvert, learning to master video marketing is a great way to start promoting your products and events. People love seeing and interacting with people on video because it feels real and personal. If you are worried about doing videos on your own, you might consider inviting a fellow distributor or a friend who is also a customer on video with you as you chat about new products. Doing this once or twice might be a great way to help you warm up to the idea of being on camera without feeling like all of the spotlight is on you.

Another way to grow used to video marketing is to start by just using stories. Facebook and Instagram story features allow you to upload 10-second video clips of you talking about a product, showing off a new product, or showing your excitement for the product that you are using. Also, they are not live so you can redo the film as many times as you desire before hitting "send."

If you want to begin moving into live videos and video marketing but are worried about doing so, starting a Facebook group and inviting your friends and family to join is a great way to begin. There, you can do videos just in front of those who you already feel comfortable in front of. Then, as this becomes more comfortable for you, you can begin moving into doing it on your personal page or your Facebook business page.

Create Content Specifically for Your Ideal Client

Since most businesses are conducted online these days, learning how to market directly to your ideal client is important. The online marketplace is massive, so marketing to the right client is essential. There is a saying in the marketing world that goes, "If you are not specific about who you are talking to, then you are talking to no one." This is completely true. Knowing how to market to the specific demographic that you want to sell to is imperative if you are going to successfully reach and attract new prospects who are actually interested in what you are selling.

Creating ideal content comes from knowing who your demographic is. Since you are already with a network marketing company or an MLM company, all you need to do is perform a quick web search to discover who the company's general demographic is. If the demographic is broad, such as "women in their 30s," focus on choosing a more specific niche for yourself. For example, say you are selling a healthy coffee that can support them in having greater energy and burning more fat. You might consider targeting "mothers in their 30s" or "busy businesswomen in their 30s." Picking a more specific audience will ensure that you are marketing to a specific person. This is how you are going to be able to pick and write relatable content, appeal to your audience better, and attract prospects. If you try marketing to the entire demographic, you are going to end up sounding confused and attempting to appeal to far too many people with completely different reasons as to why they might be interested in your product. Rather than helping you attract a larger audience, this will simply confuse your potential audience and drive them away to someone who is being more specific and intentional about their target prospect.

Once you know who you are talking to, you can begin creating content that caters specifically to those individuals. To do so, you want to focus on two things: speaking with the same type of language that they speak with and referencing the same types of experiences that they are likely to have. When you speak in a way that your audience can relate to, they are far more likely to pay attention to you and listen to what you have to say. Then, all you need to do is share regularly.

Make sure that as you share, you share a variety of things. Many of your posts should be focused solely on creating connections and showing people into your life. Remember: you want to give people the opportunity to learn about who you are, how they can relate to you, and how your products or business opportunity may fit into their lifestyle. This is how you are going to come across as human and interactive and build relationships so that people are more interested in and attracted to your opportunity.

Attend Events That Your Audience Would Attend

When it comes to bringing your products or services to events, always make sure that you are attending events that are actually relevant to what your audience would attend. Even though an event may be a great price, attending one that does not have the right audience could result in you wasting time and money. Furthermore, attending an event and having a poor turnout can feel like a blow to your self-esteem and lead to sensations of self-doubt. Instead of wasting your time and money and setting yourself up to feel bad, make sure that the only events you attend are ones that are relevant to your audience.

The same goes for online events: do not host events that your ideal audience is not likely to join. At one time in online MLM businesses, simply creating an event on Facebook and inviting a bunch of friends was enough to create a party that would earn you money. These days, doing that can result in your audience feeling annoyed because they may feel that too many people are doing this on a consistent basis. This can result in them completely ignoring you because they are tired of receiving these unsolicited invites. Instead, focus on creating a fun event and market for it. Do not invite people unless they have asked to be invited; or you have approached them, and they have agreed. This ensures that everyone joining wants to be there and is already a prospective client or recruit. In addition, this proves that you are not like other marketers and that you value people's freedom of choice. Because of this, people who say no now may say yes in the future because they do not need to worry that you will spam them with offers and sales pitches.

Show the Products in Use

Sharing pictures of your products or sales is an ineffective way to actually market to your audience. Remember: people have been doing this for a long time, and most people are annoyed with this behavior. In most cases, instead of earning you a sale, it will lose you some friends or followers online. Instead of being the person that people avoid, focus on creating an attraction marketing plan. This means that instead of sharing static pictures of a product or sales advertisements that your company created on your wall, share pictures of you actively using the products.

Anytime you receive a new shipment of products, take a few moments to hop on a video or into your stories and begin talking about the products and how they work. Do not just show pictures of the products or hold them up and talk in monotone. Instead, show how the products work. Do not be afraid to create live tutorials, sneak-peeks, and other types of content that allow you to show off how the products work in use. This is a great way to help your audience get a real insight as to what the products actually are, how they work, and why they are awesome.

You do not have to rely solely on video to share the products, either. Putting the product to work and then taking a picture and captioning about what the product is, why you love it, and how it works are also great ways to share the product in use. You can also invite your clients to share pictures or videos of them using the product as well. This can be a great way to show that you are not the only one in love with them but that those who are purchasing the products from you are, too.

As you show the products in use, rather than trying to end your show off in a hard sales pitch, simply invite people to message you if they are interested in knowing more about the product. This is a gentler way of inviting people in and is generally received better by those who you are marketing to. Creating hard sales pitches at the end of enjoyable posts can minimize the quality of them by making people instantly tune out and move on. People love to hear about how great the products that you are promoting are and how much you are loving them, but they want to feel like the idea to message you was their own and not pressured on them by you. When it comes to attraction-based marketing, the less pressure you apply, the better. Instead, show them why they need to make the choice to message you by showing off how great the products are and how much they're changing yours and your client's lives!

Don't Focus Entirely on Sales

As I mentioned above, the more you put pressure on people the more you are going to pressure them into unfollowing you or unfriending you. People are always happy to shop or learn more, but they want to feel like it was their own decision to do so. Creating regular sales pitches and constantly pushing products in people's faces is going to feel like pressure—and in the end, it will only result in you driving people away.

If you want to have more success with your direct sales business, you need to focus on creating connections and relationships with people. Remember: it is called *network* marketing, meaning that you need to *network* to market. Creating catalogues and sales images are the company's job. *Promoting* them is your job. You can do that by creating meaningful relationships with people in your network and letting them come to the idea of purchasing all on their own.

There are many ways that you can connect with your audience and build a network without coming across as spammy or annoying. They are also directly supportive of your business, meaning that doing it this way is completely worth your while. These work both online and offline.

Online, you want to show off your lifestyle. Do not just show off your lifestyle in relation to the products and services that you are offering, but show it off in general. The key, however, is to stay focused on sharing the parts of your lifestyle that are still relevant and relatable to the ones in your ideal audience. This will ensure that they are paying attention and enjoying your content. Then, those few times that you do actually post with your products and invite people to learn more about them, you are going to be seen by your audience. You will also be more well-received because you have been spending time getting to know them and building a connection with them through previous posts, so they will feel more curious about this one. Experts say that online you want 80% of your posts creating relationships with your audience and only about 20% offering sales or inviting people to learn more about your business. Keeping this ratio in your online strategy will ensure that you are staying focused on networking more so than selling.

Offline, go about life as normal. Your focus should primarily be on connecting with more people and building relationships with them. If you can encourage people to follow you on social media or connect with you somewhere online, then what ends up happening is that they build chemistry with you before learning about what you do. Then, because they like you and they already know that you do not fit the identity of a pushy salesperson, they are more likely to pay attention and grow interested when they learn about your business.

If during the conversation you have the opportunity to talk about what you do for work or you can somehow bring your products into the conversation, make sure you do so in a way that proves that there's no pressure involved. In other words, let them ask the questions. If they ask what you do for work, simply respond with the name of your company, and let them know that you are an independent distributor for them. Do not go into a long sales pitch immediately after being asked. Instead, end with that bit of information, and let them ask you if they are interested in learning more.

Chapter 6: Presenting Your Opportunity to Prospects

Knowing how to properly present your opportunity to prospects is essential. The techniques I am going to show you in this chapter are going to support you in presenting products or services to prospective clients or presenting your business opportunity to prospective recruits. Both of these will follow the same general guidelines, so simply adjust your choice of words to accommodate for the presentation that you are making.

Invite Them to Approach You

Whenever someone shows interest in your business, always invite them to approach you. Online, this would include anyone who comments on your posts expressing interest. Offline, this would include anyone who expresses interest through a conversation that the two of you share together. After the initial interest has been expressed, always invite that person to contact you in a more private forum. Online, this could be moving the conversation to a private message. Offline, this could be calling you later or meeting for coffee for a more formal get together regarding the opportunity.

Inviting your prospect to approach you shows that you are not pushy and that the next move is in their hands. This allows them to feel in control and trust that you are not going to start spamming them with your offers and trying to push your product down their throat.

When you do invite them to approach you, particularly if the invite was made in person, always give them an idea of when you are generally available. This will not only give them the opportunity to contact you on their own terms but will also get an idea of when they could contact you in their mind. Then, they are already thinking about when to call you, so they are more likely to do so. This is a great way to invite a person to more conversation in a way that is not too passive but not too pressured, either.

Let Them Ask the Questions

During the conversation that you share with your prospect, let them ask the questions. You do not want your prospect to feel like you are interrogating them, so only ask questions if they are to support you in better answering your prospect's questions. For example, if they ask which product or service would be best for them, spend some time asking questions to learn more about what their needs are. Then, give them the solution.

If the conversation starts and continues with you asking all the questions, your prospect is going to start feeling overwhelmed. They do not want to be pitched on the idea; they want to explore it. Being pitched feels uncomfortable and carries too much pressure behind it. However, if you leave them open to explore the opportunity, and if you simply give answers as they ask or make yourself available to help them through their exploration, they feel in control. This helps them feel more comfortable and as though they are being respected by you during the process. As a result, they will remain interested and open to learning more about what you have to offer.

Lead The Conversation without Pressure

Although you want to let your prospect ask all of the questions, you still want to lead the conversation. After all, you are the expert. Gently guiding them toward the answers they need to purchase or join you is the best way to guide the conversation but without making it feel overwhelming. You can do this by offering answers that directly answer their question but begin guiding them to new thoughts that work toward the finalizing of the sale or recruitment.

For example, say your customer asks: "How do I know which financial solution is best for me?" You could answer, "Well, that really depends on what your needs are! Can you give me more information on what you feel you need most from your finances?" Then, when they give you their answer, you may begin telling them about how they can have those needs met by your solutions.

Guiding someone toward the solution rather than pushing them toward it will support you in closing more deals. This is because you are attracting them to the solution, making it seem more interesting and fulfilling to them. Furthermore, this form of guidance gives you plenty of opportunities to learn more about what their needs are and what solutions they would actually benefit from. Finding people the right solution is just as important as closing the opportunity, as this will ensure that they are satisfied with their choice after the deal is closed. That way, they are more likely to feel positive about it, and they will come back for more as a result.

Subtly Create a Sense of Urgency

When it comes to marketing you, always want to create a sense of urgency that encourages people to make a decision sooner rather than later. This is how you ensure that people continue thinking about you and that they do not simply forget because the offer was too passive or "it will be available later when I'm more ready."

Creating a subtle sense of urgency is how you can show people that there is urgency there but without creating pressure on them. For example, "Our September incentive ends in three days, so make sure you choose quickly!" is too much pressure. This is going to result in people feeling overwhelmed and likely looking for reasons to back out or purposefully wait longer just so that they can get away from the feeling of being pressured. Instead, say something like, "We still have three days left before this great incentive ends, so why don't you take a couple of days to think it over? Do you mind if I message you back in a day or two to see if you have any more questions I can answer for you?" This sentence proves the urgency of the offer in a way that lacks pressure and includes a request to follow up with your prospect. This means that they will spend more time thinking about it, will feel as though they are in control, and will look forward to hearing back from you so that you can help them make their decision.

Have a Resource Available for Them to Read Over

One great way to really help encourage prospects to purchase or join you is to have something for them to look at while they are thinking things through. A small handout, a write-up, a video, or any other form of resource that they can read over to learn more while they think things through is great. This resource should answer any basic questions they may have and give them the rundown on why the opportunity is one worth going for.

Giving people a resource is not only a great way to help them think things through, but it is also a wonderful no-pressure way to get information into their hands. This means that rather than going away and simply being left to their own thinking devices or having to look for other resources (and potentially find someone with more who communicates better with them,) they can look at yours. This keeps them operating as your prospect and interested in learning more from you and coming back to do business through you. As a result, you and your opportunity both stay fresh in their mind, making it more likely for them to choose in favor of closing the deal.

Always Request to Follow Up

Every single time you have a conversation with a prospect, always ask if you can follow up with them in a couple of days. This ensures that they are open to further communication and puts the power of the follow up in your hands. If you leave it in your prospects hands, they can easily forget, and then you lose a prospect. If you follow up too soon after not having set a clear expectation on if and when you would do so, then this follow-up can seem spammy. Instead, setting the expectations and taking the responsibility for the follow-up ensures that you are the one who will reach out. Through this, your prospect knows exactly when they can expect one, or they can adjust the date of when the follow-up would be accordingly.

When you take the responsibility for the follow-up, make sure that you always do just that. Never present your opportunity to a prospect and set the intention of a follow-up and then forget to do so. This can cost you a prospect and result in you not successfully closing the deal. Write the person's name down in your calendar on the date that the follow-up needs to happen, and make sure that you show up. This will ensure that you are readily available to continue presenting any information that they need to support them in making their decision.

Chapter 7: Converting Prospects into Distributors or Customers

After you have gotten to the point in the conversation where you are ready to start making your actual sales pitch, it is important that you do so in the right way. You do not want to spend plenty of time working toward creating a strong reputation with someone and building rapport only to blow it during the conversion.

There are various things that you need to take into consideration when it comes to converting prospects into distributors or customers. In this chapter, I am going to show you how to make the pitch itself and how to make sure that you are pitching the right thing that will adequately serve that person's needs. That way, you can make the conversion and do so with a solution that actually fulfills that prospect's needs, ensuring that they are satisfied and eager to continue on with the chosen solution and beyond.

Spend Time Getting to Know Your Pitch

It is always important that you have an idea of what you want to pitch to your prospect before you actually go into the conversation. If you are about to go into a follow-up conversation, spend the time between the initial point of contact and the follow-up curating a pitch specifically for that person. For the times where you need to pitch on the spot without a follow-up, have some form of pitch already practiced so that you know how to talk to the prospect without stumbling.

Spending time developing your pitch and getting to know it really well will ensure that when the time comes to actually make the pitch, you're ready. The worst thing you can do is go into a pitch unprepared and fumble over your words, apply too much or too little pressure, or leave information out because you were ill-prepared. Practicing in advance or at least making a mental note of what points you want to cover will ensure that you know exactly what you want to say and that you are ready to say it.

Early on, no matter how much you practice your pitch, it may still feel awkward. Furthermore, practicing a pitch without any experience as to what types of questions or statements people might have can be a challenge. As a result, some of your earliest pitches may not be your best work. Still, use this as an opportunity to get to know the pitch and to look for opportunities to make your pitch more effectively in the future. Make a note of what questions people typically have, what objections you are running into the most, and any other considerations that you feel you need to note in order to make your pitch effectively. Then, in the future, adjust your pitches to accommodate for these unique changes.

The more you practice, the easier it will be for you to curate pitches on the spot. This will come as a result of having a stronger idea of what the answers are to people's questions, feeling more confident in yourself, and having more practice in learning how to overcome common objections. As you grow more practiced, your pitches will become more candid and effective, which means you will begin getting greater results.

Even though you already know that your earliest pitches may not be your best ones, it is imperative that you prepare and practice. You have to start somewhere, and there is only one way that you can get better at something. Be prepared to pitch, and be prepared to do so often. This is an essential part of growth, so using this tool and leveraging it effectively will ensure that you achieve great results.

Initiate the Conversation with a Question

You never want to jump straight into the pitch when you are selling something to someone. This comes across as pushy and tacky. It also shows that you are not considerate about the other person's concerns. This can leave a bad impression on people, resulting in a quick and immediate "no" and a damaged reputation.

Instead, start the conversation with a question. If you are following up with someone who you have already chatted with and who has already been considering the opportunity, open with something like "Hey (name)! I'm just following up from the other day. Have you had a chance to think about (opportunity) yet?" This is a simple conversation starter that gets the conversation immediately focused on what you are working toward without sounding pushy or inconsiderate.

If you haven't had a conversation yet with the person, and this is your first one, you want to start the conversation with a question that gets the person thinking and talking about your opportunity. Something like "Hey (name)! I see that you are interested in (opportunity), and I just wanted to reach out and see if there were any questions you might have about it?" This is a simple and open question that invites the person to ask about anything they may be curious about. As a result, the conversation gets started, and the ball gets rolling so that you can eventually move into your pitch.

Answer Any Questions Your Prospect Might Have

Before you *ever* make a pitch to *anyone*, make sure you have the information that you need to do so. If you are not considerate about your prospect, you are not going to convert them into a distributor or customer. It simply won't happen. People like to do business with people who are considerate and compassionate, not people who are pushy and who seem like they are just trying to close a deal.

Instead of prematurely making your pitch, take some time, and get to know the person and their needs. Pay attention to what matters to them, what they are looking for, and what can really support them in making a decision. Ask them if they have any questions, and make it clear that they are always welcome to come to you if they need support or are looking for more answers. Serving your prospects instead of selling to your prospects will ensure that they feel accommodated for and considered. As a result, they will realize that you are compassionate and genuinely interested in creating great results for them using your opportunity.

Only once you know that you already have all of the information and that they have asked all of their outstanding questions should you then move into a pitch. However, you do not want to accidentally draw the question period out too long before you move into the pitch. Doing that could result in them losing interest and not paying attention, or talking themselves out of it altogether.

The best way to tell that someone is ready to be pitched to is by the amount of interest they have in your opportunity and the initiative that they are showing. If they are asking you more about the products and are showing interest in hearing about the opportunity, then you can begin pitching. Alternatively, if they begin answering questions with similar answers or by tying them back into other answers (i.e. saying things like, "as I said before…"), then you know that you want to move toward the pitch so that you don't bore them or make them feel like you are not listening.

Even after you are confident that your prospect has asked all of their questions, always make it clear that they can come to you at any time if they have more concerns. This includes during the process, afterward, or at any time in the future. Letting them know that you are always available to support them helps them feel confident that if they have anything else that they desire to ask, you will be there to support them in finding the answers they need. This shows that you are service-based and focused on giving them the best experience possible, making your prospect feel supported and cared for and more likely to want to do business with you again.

Make Your Pitch

Once everything else has been done, you are ready to make your pitch. Here is where you want to begin using what you had already practiced. That way, you make sure that you have included all of the information required to support your prospect in making their official decision.

When you open the pitch, always make it clear that you have been listening to their needs and that you feel you have a great opportunity or offer that is going to fulfill what they are looking for. Then, let them know what the opportunity is and why you think it would fit their needs. End your pitch with a question that invites them to engage back with you so that the pitch does not sound like the end of a conversation.

It is important that you do not make your pitch too long or drawn out. Using what is called an "elevator" pitch is a great way to begin pitching your opportunity to people because it supports you in giving just enough information and then only giving more when your prospect shows interest in knowing more. These pitches generally start with one to two lines about the opportunity, followed by a question. Then, if they ask for more information, you can add in more and let them know further details about the opportunity.

Below is a great example of how you can make a pitch to recruit someone using the elevator pitch style.

> *You*: "You mentioned that you are looking for a way to earn extra income so that you can cover your bills easier, and I know that you are passionate about health. The company I am with offers incredible health products that can support people in achieving their wellness goals and feeling more empowered about their health. I really think this would tie in great with your needs and passions! Does this opportunity interest you?"

Prospect: "Yes, that does sound like a great idea!"

> *You:* "Great! The company is seriously incredible; I know you will love it! Right now, we have an exclusive offer to join the company for just $99! With that, you get all of the marketing materials you need to get started, plus some great products for you to share with your market. I also have a great online community where I offer training and support to distributors with goals just like yours! Would you like me to send you the sign-up link and help you get started?"

Prospect: "Yes please!"

As you can see, formatting the pitch in this way supports the person in getting information but without feeling overloaded. If you were to go too far into detail with information by sending every single detail over right away, you might overwhelm your prospect and leave them not wanting to answer you. Instead, giving only the information that is relevant to the point of the conversation that you are at can support you in making the pitch in a way that keeps your prospect engaged and interested. Then, they can make the decision, and you can offer to help walk them through the process if they choose to join you!

The same general concept goes to selling products. While you will not be making the pitch based on the business opportunity, you will be making it based on the product or service that your prospect is interested in. Presenting the information in the same way but based on your product or service offer will ensure that your prospect has the information that they need to make their decision and that you can close the deal.

Chapter 8: Creating A Strong Follow-Up System

Following up with people is an essential way of making sure that every single lead you generate is tapped. If you spend all of your time marketing and generating new leads, and then you do not take the time to actually follow up with those leads, you are wasting your time. Many potential customers or distributors can slip through your fingers and find their way to another distributor if you are not paying attention and making use of a strong follow-up system.

Creating a follow-up system does not have to be challenging or overdone. Instead, a simple follow-up system can be created that makes it easy to follow and effective. In fact, when it comes to a follow-up system, the easier it is, the more effective it becomes. I am going to show you how you can take advantage of both automatic and manual follow-up systems to ensure that you successfully follow up with every single lead that you generate. Making use of both of these styles will ensure that no one slips through the cracks and that you are regularly nurturing your leads so that your network continues to grow and convert.

When to Use Automated Follow-ups

Automated follow-ups are a great way to follow up with people who enjoy following your online presence and who opt in to staying up to date. The most common way to do automated follow-ups is through using an e-mail list.

Your automated follow-up system is going to come into use anytime someone lands on your website or is directed to sign up to your newsletter by you in the online space. For example, if you have a blog, you can capture emails on it through a pop-up that encourages people to sign up for your email newsletter. Alternatively, if you are on Facebook, you might consider leaving a link where people can sign up to stay up to date and receive great information regarding your industry and the products or services that you offer. Some companies have newsletters that have already been designed for you and that are sent out by your company from anyone who signs up on your consultant website. These can be great, as they capture emails and put them directly into a list and cover the marketing part for you so that you don't have to. However, they are created by the company themselves, so they will lack your personal branding and tone of voice.

Using email lists is a great way to allow people to choose to be followed up with and to continue receiving follow-ups to their inbox every time a new newsletter goes out. These types of prospects are willingly choosing to be followed up with and are opting to see the new newsletter each time it comes out. As a result, they are considered to be warm leads because they are showing so much interest in your opportunity.

When to Use Manual Follow-ups

Manual follow-ups are the best way to follow up on a more personal level. This is how you can follow up with someone whom you have already chatted with about your opportunity and who wants to know more about what you have to offer. You can follow up with people manually any time you have had a personal conversation with them.

Using manual follow-ups is more intimate and focused specifically on the person that you are following up with. Through this type of follow-up, you have the unique opportunity to answer questions and make yourself personally available to your prospect so that you can support them in making their decision. Manual follow-ups are a great way to generate hot leads because these are people who are asking you to update them. As a result, they are more likely to purchase from you. Furthermore, you can curate your information and pitch just for them, making it more effective for that person specifically. When you have the opportunity to do so, always use manual follow up with individual people. That way, you have more control over the situation, and you can close the deal with greater ease.

How to Create an Automated Follow-up System

Setting up an automated follow-up system requires three aspects: a lead-generator, a place where you capture emails, and a platform from which you send your emails. With these three components in place, you have everything you need to encourage people to opt-in and to receive your newsletters through their emails.

Lead-generators or opt-in incentives are something that people offer as a way to encourage them to sign up for their email list. If you choose to make a lead-generator, which you absolutely should, you want to make something that is going to be relevant to your audience. A short e-book, a workbook, a checklist, an exclusive training video, or any other form of inexpensive but valuable freebie that you can offer is a great way to give people an incentive to join your mailer list.

Once they have joined, the person should then receive the item directly to their inbox, or they should land on the page where the freebie is offered. Most web hosting companies like WordPress or Squarespace, as well email newsletter platforms like MailChimp or ConvertKit, will give you all of the tools that you need to ensure that your new subscriber receives their promised gift. They should also be able to walk you through the process of creating your opt-in page or pop up so that people have a spot where they can opt-in for your freebie and receive your newsletter.

Lastly, all you need to do is create great email newsletters and send them out on a regular basis! For automated newsletters, ideally, you want to be sending a new email once per week. This way, you can update your subscribers on weekly deals, give them great new tips or advice that is specific to your niche, and invite them to message you back. When you email your subscribers once per week, you ensure that you are not overwhelming them so that they unsubscribe and you also ensure that you are emailing them enough that they actually remember who you are and what offer you have for them.

How to Create a Manual Follow-up System

Manual follow-up systems are extremely simple. Essentially, you want to get the person's best method of contact and write it down. Then, make sure you write down their name, too. You can also include a note on how to pronounce it if it is a particularly challenging name so that you do not accidentally mispronounce it during your follow-up. Then, you need to note in your calendar what date you need to update them on.

It is also a good idea to write down some notes regarding what it is that you are following up on and what their particular needs or concerns are. This ensures that you do not forget about what they have already told you and that you are readily prepared to go into the follow-up conversation. This also proves that they matter enough to you, that you took the time to remember their needs and to pay attention to what they have told you.

Since manual follow up is quite straightforward, there really is nothing special that you need to know other than to write down their information and then get in touch with them when you have promised to. This is definitely the simplest form of follow-up, though it can be time-consuming if you have many people to update.

Make sure that, if for some reason, you cannot follow up on the date that you agreed you would, at least make contact with that person. Do not simply leave them waiting. If you can, give them a quick call or message, and ask how they have been doing and if they've had a chance to think things over. If they respond that they have, rather than going into the pitch or using this particular follow-up to move into the offer, use it to book your next follow-up. That way, your prospect knows that you have not forgotten about them and can look forward to connecting with you again. Leaving a prospect without answers and not connecting with them when you said you would leave a bad impression about how you do business. It can also result in them not wanting to do business with you for fear of being abandoned or not having access to the support that they need.

Knowing When to Stop Following Up

Sometimes, you might find yourself following up with someone who seems to be going nowhere. They may have initially been a prospect—but after a few attempted follow-ups, the conversation seems to go nowhere, or they are showing a lack of interest in what you are offering. If this happens, it is important that you know when to stop following up with them. Generally, after three follow-ups that do not advance to anything more than disinterested conversation or with a conversation that feels like you have to put too much work into to get any answers from the other person, you can stop.

Following up with someone who is disinterested too many times can result in them growing annoyed with you and unfollowing or unfriending you. Furthermore, it is a waste of your time, as it will not result in anything positive. Even if you do eventually get them to make up their mind and purchase from you or join you, the amount of work that you are going to have to put into keeping them is going to be too much. Plus, if they join you, they will be unlikely to do anything with their opportunity because they simply are not motivated enough. Instead of wasting your time following up with people who are not interested, move on to people who genuinely are.

Chapter 9: Building an Effective Downline

Since a large part of your income in MLM is based on your downline and their performance, knowing how to build an effective downline is important. You need to make sure that you are finding the right prospects who are actually going to take advantage of the business opportunity and turn it into something successful for themselves and for you.

In this chapter, I am going to show you how to qualify prospects to discover who is going to be a strong downline support and who is going to stay most dedicated to their goals. Finding downlines who are qualified in this way will ensure that you are finding people who are committed to success. As a result, your whole team will grow more powerful.

Finding Prospects for Your Downline

Part of building your downline is knowing where to find prospects. Prospects can come from all over the place, though the most common place to find prospects is on social media. Through your engagement and attraction marketing efforts, people are naturally going to start looking toward you to learn more about the opportunity that you have to offer them. The more you share about yourself and how your company is changing your life, the more your prospects are going to start showing up and seeking information from you about joining your company.

The best way to continue searching for prospects is to continue posting and to engage with every single person who interacts with your posts. If you have people who tend to engage a great deal or who show interest, do the same and begin engaging more on their posts, too. This helps you develop a relationship with that person, which is going to help set the tone for you to attract them to your business even more.

When people start noticing how much your business is changing your life and how much fun you are having, they are going to start asking you questions about the opportunity. Then, all you have to do is have your initial and follow-up conversation, and then give them your pitch to get them on board. This is quite simple. In fact, it is the easiest way to get new prospects joining your company.

People who approach you and who put this level of initiative into joining your company are the ones who are most likely to be self-starters. This proves that they are going to be willing to do what it takes to generate success and achieve their goals in the MLM industry. As a result, they are more likely to remain active consultants who will help your own position within the company grow as they continue to grow as well.

Another way that you can meet prospects is through gaining referrals. If you have clients whom you love and who have been purchasing from you for a while, ask them if they are willing to refer their friends to you that might be interested in what you are doing. If they have any friends who show interest in your industry or in making extra money, then, they can refer them to you, and you can show them the opportunity.

Prospects can show up virtually anywhere, too. You never know when you are going to have a conversation with a person who is going to be interested in doing something like you are doing. Always keep your eyes open for an opportunity to let someone know that you have an offer they might be interested in. Then, give them the information that they need to contact you, and invite them to do just that. Remember: you do not want to be pushy, but you always want to make sure that you are putting the offer out there.

Engaging with Your Prospective Downline

Once you have met someone who might be interested in becoming a part of your team, it is a good idea that you begin engaging with your prospect. This is a great way to begin getting to know who they are, so as to get an idea of what their interests and goals are, and to discover if they would actually be a good fit to your company. You can also use this time to let them know more, too, to see if they feel interested as well.

As you engage with your prospective downline, make sure that you are taking the time to sell them on the idea. You do not want to approach the subject too passively, or this can result in them thinking that the idea is not worth their time or excitement. Instead, share some success stories with them, and let them know how much there is to be excited about. This is a great way to show them that there is plenty to look forward to within the business should they choose to join.

You can also focus on sharing how helpful your team is and how easy it is to succeed when you have so many people working together to help you. This is something that many people look forward to with MLM businesses. Oftentimes, people joining MLM companies have never run their own business before. As a result, the idea of having to do everything on their own may seem intimidating or scary. Letting them know that there is a strong system of support awaiting them is a great way to prove that they will not have to do everything on their own. Focus on emphasizing how close your team is and how much they truly do help each other work toward succeeding in achieving their own goals.

Make sure that as you are sharing this conversation with your prospect that you allow the conversation to follow a natural path. You do not want it to seem like the only thing you can talk about is the opportunity. Let them know that you are a real human and that you have other interests, too. If they steer the conversation toward something like hobbies or family, for example, do not be afraid to follow the conversation down that route. Then, after a few sentences back and forth on that subject, find a way to tie it back into the opportunity. For example, you could bring it back to the topic of your business by mentioning how you being with this company has impacted your family.

It is important that you spend just as much time building a relationship with prospects as you do selling them on the opportunity. If they are joining you, chances are one of the biggest reasons is because they want to be able to earn more money and have access to the support that comes with being with an MLM company. Prove that there is plenty of support, personal connection, and training involved by being willing to show them that right from the very start.

One thing people tend to do wrong is starting relationships out on the wrong foot. Your first impression truly does matter. You want to develop a reputation of being someone who cares and who puts people first, rather than someone who is simply trying to recruit as many people as possible. When people realize how compassionate you are and how much you care about the work you do, they will be far more likely to join you.

Qualifying Your Downline to Find the Best Team Members

While you probably won't want to deny anyone who asks to join your team, it is a good idea that you take the time to qualify the prospects that you want to pursue your team. Qualifying your prospects is the best way to make sure that you are building your team up with inspiring, empowering, and motivated people who are going to do their best to generate success with their business. It also ensures that you do not waste your time trying to recruit people who are not going to do anything with the opportunity anyway, as they do not end up earning your team any growth or income in the end.

Qualifying people requires you to look for four main characteristics in each person that you are pursuing to join your team: drive, goals, a positive personality, and the ability to connect with other people. When a person has these four characteristics then you can guarantee that they already have a great deal of what it takes to succeed. With the right training and support, these are the types of prospects who go on to become team leaders that rapidly climb the ranks and generate success for themselves.

These are the people that are going to take what you give them and run with it, so they are the ones that you want to be investing your time into. Not only are you going to have the blessing of watching your own business grow, then, but you will also get to watch someone else's. When you are operating a company that relies so much on having a team, such as with an MLM company, seeing your entire team succeed is exciting and inspiring. This will motivate you to do better, and it will motivate them to do better as well. As a result, you all get to win because each of you is taking the time required to invest in yourselves and your businesses.

Chapter 10: Leading Your Team Members Effectively

Knowing how to lead your downline is an important process of building your business. Having a strong team is a part of what makes working with an MLM company so attractive. People love having that support and community and knowing that they can rely on others who are working towards similar goals as they are. Having people that they can relate to and develop connections within this way inspires them to continue working and to stay motivated in achieving their goals.

If you want to generate the type of team that stays focused on success and that continues moving forward, you need to set the tone and be the person that guides the team in this direction. You can do this by developing a service-based leadership that is going to allow you to show up and is there to support your team. This will also help your team grow into the team culture that you are developing through your leadership, ensuring that everyone contributes to the supportive, compassionate, and motivating environment that you are building for them.

The Importance of Service-Based Leadership

Service-based leadership is one that is designed to stay focused on how you can help your team do better. Rather than simply leading in the way that you believe leadership is needed, you lead in a manner that your team needs you to lead. Being a service-based leader means that you need to stay receptive to your team's feedback so that you can continue leading in a way that serves them.

When you lead in a service-based leadership style, only three things remain consistent: support, communication, and adaptation. Your primary focus should always revolve around supporting your team to do better so that they can build their businesses and continue to achieve success. This helps them stay motivated and committed, keeping them working at their businesses for a long time to come. You can maintain this level of support by communicating frequently. When you communicate often, you can listen to their needs and make yourself available as needed. Lastly, you need to know how to adapt. The needs of your team will change from time to time, and you need to know how to adapt your leadership style and approach to ensure that you fulfill these needs as they change. As long as you continue working to support, communicate with, and adapt to your team's needs, you can guarantee that your downline is going to grow strong and unstoppable.

'Be A Leader, Not a Boss

When it comes to leading a team it is essential that you learn to be a leader and not a boss. Remember: these individuals are all people who, like you, want to do their own thing. They value their freedom, the feeling of being in control, and their right to do things their way. This is one of the big attractions of network marketing. That being said, do not be the person that tries to take that away by attempting to lead your team like you are their boss. You are not. You are their leader.

The best way you can lead people is to show them through your own actions and to coach them when it is needed. When you are a role model that they can look up to, your downline can easily look to you for support and inspiration. They will want to come to you for assistance because they will trust that they can get support from you when it is needed. Your downline will also know that when they seek you out, they are going to be shown how to do things, not told. This means that they are going to really get the opportunity to learn how to do their best so that they can achieve the same type of success that you are aiming for. Remember: you are all here to be your own bosses. Lead your team so that they know how to be the best boss to themselves that they can be.

Learn How to Manage Your Time

As your team continues to grow, the demands on your time will continue to grow as well. Learning how to effectively manage your time from the start is a powerful way to make sure that you are never wasting time, losing time, or running out of time. Every single conversation you have with a member of your team should be productive and focused. Stay clear on what the point of the conversation is, and stay on topic. The more focused you are, the easier it is to reach your goal and move on to your next order of business.

This also goes for when you are doing training calls, orientations, and other similar events. If you are in any forum where you are talking to a large number of people all at once, make sure that you stay on topic and that you are clearly focused on your results. Getting off topic or taking too long to communicate the point to your audience will bore them and result in them not listening to you. If they stop listening, you're not leading effectively. Be the type of leader who gets to the point, not the one who loses everyone's interest and fails to lead.

Stay Consistent in Your Leadership

As you develop your leadership style, make sure that you stay consistent. Your team will not appreciate having you being unreliable and inconsistent when they are trying to look up to you for support and motivation. Be consistent in the tasks you do as a leader, in the training you offer, and in the way that you motivate and inspire people. Show up every single day, and give the same level of commitment (or more) every single day. This shows people that you are dedicated and motivated and that they can rely on you.

You also want to make sure that you are training your downline on the importance of consistency. Teach them how to take baby steps towards generating success rather than pushing them to try and sprint to the finish line. Running a business requires time and patience, so demonstrating this and teaching it to your downline is important. If you want, you can create a resource that outlines the baby steps they need to be taking to succeed and offer it to each person in your downline. Then, they each have access to what they need so that they know what step to take next and where to go in each moment.

Keep The Lines of Communication Open

Nothing is more challenging than trying to work with a leader who is unapproachable or does not communicate with their team. When you are leading your team, make sure that you keep your lines of communication open. This allows your team to know that there is support available to them whenever they need it.

As your downline grows, you might find that making yourself available around the clock is virtually impossible. Trying to get back to that many people or trying to stay up to date with everyone can be a challenge. Still, communication is important. In this situation, there are a few things that you can do to maintain your open communication but without taking away from your own time or overwhelming your schedule too much. The first one is to have set days or hours that you are available to share with your downline. This is when they can contact you or expect a response from you if they have contacted you. That way, everyone knows when you are available and does not grow frustrated or annoyed if you do not message them outside of those times.

Another thing that you can do if your team is growing particularly large is to have a set day or days each week that you will go live on your team's Facebook group and invite your downline to join you. Then, they can ask questions, and you can update them on anything that is going on in the business through that video. This is a great way to show your team your face and let them know that a real person is leading their team. It builds relationships between you and your team members and keeps the communication open.

Lastly, if your team is too big for you to lead alone, you might consider picking a couple of other leaders on your team to help you lead the team. Picking people who know the company well, who have shown the initiative, and who are leading their own downlines is a great way to make sure that you have enough people available to help anyone who may have questions. Make sure that your entire team knows who is being added to the leadership and that there is a document or note available somewhere that lets them know how they can contact leaders and if any of the leaders have a set time when they are able to be contacted. This way, everyone knows who to go to and when.

Encourage Your Downline to Leverage Their Strengths

When it comes to leading people, it is essential that you teach people how to recognize their strengths and leverage them for their businesses. Inspiring people to see how great they are and how successful they are with certain activities is an incredible way to motivate people and keep them moving forward.

In addition to having people come to know their own strengths, take the time to recognize their strengths, too. Watch your downline in action, and do not be afraid to celebrate them for their achievements. Write posts in your team group about how awesome they are, highlighting their achievements, or celebrating them for doing a job well done. There isn't a need to be any special occasion for celebrating people. Simply celebrating people just because is a great way to keep the team's morale up and positivity pumping so that everyone stays motivated to do their best.

As people grow to know and leverage their strengths, they will also come to understand what their weaknesses are. Then, if need be, you can coach them on how to overcome these weaknesses so that they can continue to develop a strong business. If you notice that many people share a similar weakness, you might consider doing specific training on how they can overcome these weaknesses so that they can experience greater success.

Train, Inspire, and Motivate

As a leader, the best things that you can offer to your downline is training, inspiration, and motivation. Make sure that these three things are included in how you lead your team. Focus on leading them with the intention of showing them how they can do their best, inspiring them to feel confident in their ability to do their best, and motivating them to put the effort into proving to themselves that they can make it happen.

A great way to keep these three components active in your team is to include them in your specific leadership schedule. In other words, every week or month have some form of training in the group where you or another leader will come on and train the rest of the group on how to do something. This does not necessarily have to be someone who is leading your team, either.

Inviting any team member who has something to teach or even inviting guest speakers to chat with your team is a great way to begin building up your team and teaching them how to do their best. Make sure that these trainings always include motivation and inspiration, too, to encourage your team to keep moving forward.

Chapter 11: Handling Rejection like a Pro

Rejection is an inevitable part of a business. At the end of the day, no matter how awesome your offer is or how much you think it would work for someone else, some people just won't be interested. When you experience rejection in your business, it is essential that you handle it properly. Handled properly, rejection is not necessarily the means to an end. Instead, it may be an opportunity to prove that you have integrity and that you can respect others. As a result, the person who have rejected you may just become the same person who refers your next best prospect to you.

Detach from the Outcome Before You Even Start

If you go into every single prospect or presentation with an attachment to how you think it is going to turn out, then chances are you are going to feel a lot more hurt when things don't work out. Instead of setting yourself up to feel bad every time something doesn't work out, set yourself up to succeed. Detach from the outcome, and let things flow naturally.

Detaching from the outcome ensures that you are not so fixated on your desired results, that you end up too narrow sighted to see other opportunities that may arise, too. When you go into anything with an attachment toward how you want it to end, you can pretty much guarantee that you are going to experience being let down in one way or another. You will either feel disappointed in the rejection itself or not realize that many opportunities came of it, or you will be so fixed on having your outcome, that you may not realize that an even better one presented itself. As a result, you can miss out on many opportunities that actually could pan out because you are too busy worrying about what hadn't.

When you go into anything, rather than having an attachment to the outcome, set a goal. When you do, set the goal loosely. Set an intention that you are going to get the best results possible and that these results are, in one way or another, going to support your business growing to be bigger than it already is. This ensures that you head into every single opportunity with a clear mind and a focus on having the best possible outcome, rather than a specific one.

Consider Asking Why They Rejected Your Offer

Whenever someone rejects your offer or opportunity, never be afraid to ask why. Asking for the reason is a great way to discover if there was anything that you could have done differently or anything that you should have paid attention to beforehand. Feedback is always a great way to discover where you can do better, how you can grow, and how you can emphasize your success.

When you do ask for someone to let you know why they have rejected your offer, make sure that you go into it ready to receive feedback. You might end up learning that something you did was the very reason why they said no in the end. This can feel painful because you never want to think that you made a mistake that cost you a prospect. However, realize that in taking the time to listen to this feedback, you can learn how to approach your sales more effectively so that you will have an easier time recruiting new prospects in the future.

Sometimes, people may not want to offer you feedback, or the feedback that they offer you might be unproductive or even unkind. In these situations, do not press for more information or get into an argument with the other person. Instead, end the conversation, and release what they have said. This will allow you to let go of the situation and move on so that you can continue growing your business. If what a person says results in you feeling unmotivated or discouraged, take this time to practice your mindset skills so that you can give yourself a pep talk and move on.

Refrain from Investing Your Emotions into It

When it comes to business, people rarely make decisions based on their emotions. Instead, they make them based off of ration, reason, and logic. Make sure that you do not come into decisions very emotionally invested. Doing so can result in you feeling personally invested in the outcome and emotionally involved to the point that it feels like a personal attack on you when people reject you. As a consequence, you may find yourself feeling very emotional after any rejection.

While you do not want to run your business with a lack of passion, you also want to refrain from becoming so emotionally invested, that it is a challenge for you to remain level-headed and focused when challenges come up. Instead, be invested enough that you can show off your passion but be detached enough that your emotions do not feel personally attacked anytime someone rejects you.

In addition, you also want to refrain from bringing your emotions into any business dealing to avoid having any emotional outbursts. If you are particularly emotionally invested in an outcome, handling rejection can be much harder. People who do not check their emotions properly can end up having an argument or another unprofessional outburst with someone, which can result in you not only losing the prospect but also losing your reputation. If you handle rejection in this way, people are going to think that you are unprofessional and not a good person to do business with. Instead of looking for your support, they will be afraid that you will have the same response toward them.

Do Not Look at Rejection as a Means to an End

Rejection is not always the means to an end. In fact, in most cases, rejection can be seen as a positive thing. When someone rejects you and then the two of you never share an interaction again, in many cases, you have been given a blessing. Someone who wants to reject you but chooses to join you because they are afraid of saying no can end up being a waste of time in the end. This has nothing to do with the person or their character but rather the fact that they are not the type of prospect that's going to help generate more success within your business.

Another thing to realize is that when you get rejected, this does not mean that the person does not think your product has value or is interesting. Instead, it simply means that they are not interested themselves. Perhaps it does not fit in with their lifestyle or budget, so they decide that they are not interested. However, if you respect them and you treat that person with dignity and kindness, you can feel confident that if they do meet someone who would be interested, they might just refer them your way. That's right—the very people who reject you might be the same ones to refer some of the best clients your way. Always look on the bright side!

Handle Rejection with Poise, Grace, and Integrity

When it comes to handling rejection, always make sure that you do so with poise and grace. Consider what your reputation is and act accordingly. Use manners, show respect, and maintain your integrity during the entire conversation. Never behave in a way that makes the person question whether or not they were right to have even contacted you or given you the time to pitch in the first place. If you do, you will leave a bad impression over who you are.

They say that when it comes to business, people show their true colors when they are rejected or when they face hard times. Knowing how to handle your rejections with poise, grace, and integrity will ensure that you show people that you can handle these moments with dignity. As a result, they will have greater respect for you. This means that even though you lose a prospect, you do not lose your reputation, too.

Make Sure You Respect Yourself

In any instance of rejection, always take the time to respect yourself. If you are disrespected during the process of being rejected, or if anyone tries to treat you poorly during the process, do not take it. You are not required to argue your worth to anyone. Instead, politely end the conversation and call it a day.

Unfortunately, sometimes in business, you are going to face people who have very little respect for other people. If you do not take the time to learn how to respect yourself and apply it, you might find yourself failing in your business based on the mean words of a bully. This is a tragic way to let your business fail. Do not let the harsh words of an unkind person bring you down, and do not stoop so low as to respond to them. You owe yourself the respect of refusing that kind of treatment and moving on from the conversation. Furthermore, you are your own boss, and you have every right to demand that you be treated with respect in every single conversation. If you are not, you do not have to engage in that conversation—period. This is true even for conversations with people who are paying you or bringing money into your business. It may be challenging, but do not be afraid to stand up for yourself. You deserve it.

Chapter 12: Why Some People Don't Make Money?

Chances are that you have heard of many stories where people join MLM companies, sell for a little while, exhaust their market quickly, and then quit. It is not uncommon to have these same people tell you about how it is basically impossible to make any money with an MLM business and that you are better off doing something else. The reality is that you actually can make a great deal of money with your business. However, there are some fatal mistakes that people make that result in them not making any money. As a result, these people never succeed.

The truth is there are many people who will never make it in an MLM company. This is because they do not have what it takes. They are not devoted enough and do not have the drive to continue trying, and they are unwilling to learn about how to turn this venture into a successful and profitable source of income. This does not mean that they are bad people—just that they are not cut out for making money in the MLM industry. Making money through MLM does require you to take the time to learn about what you are actually doing and commit to doing better all the time. If you do not invest that kind of time and commitment into your business, you can pretty much guarantee that you will fail.

I want to give you the main reasons why people do not make money in MLM companies and what you can do to make sure that you are not one of these people. This way, you can feel confident that you will not make the same mistakes that they did and that you will instead be able to succeed in your business and be one of the many millionaires produced by the MLM industry.

They Don't Have Enough Focus

It is not uncommon for people to join network marketing businesses and assume that they will be easy because it is all laid out in front of them. They want their friend or acquaintance make it look easy, and they assume that they simply need to buy the kit and make a few posts—and then sales will come rolling in. When things don't happen right away, they begin to lose focus, and they quit before they've even really had a chance to get things rolling.

When you start your network marketing business, it is essential that you commit to staying focused and working on your business every single day. If your consistency falters, and you stop showing up, you can pretty much guarantee that you are going to fail in your business.

They Never Learned How to Market Properly

Unfortunately, a lot of negative and ineffective marketing strategies are promoted in MLM companies. People who are not really clear on what effective marketing strategies are teach other people how to market in a way that is unproductive. As a result, many MLM distributors end up marketing in a way that is tacky, pushy, and ineffective. Because people typically only respond poorly to these tactics if they even bother to respond at all, it can result in the distributor quitting before they ever actually got anywhere with their business.

It is essential that you understand that you are working as a professional marketer when you become a distributor. This means that you need to read up on how to market effectively and discover what it actually takes to market. This way, you can attract clients to you rather than push them away by marketing in a way that makes them annoyed and uninterested.

They Didn't Position Themselves as a Leader

As a distributor that is selling a product or service, people want to know that you know what you are talking about. If a person who is selling does not sell with authority and confidence, people are going to start assuming that their products are probably not that great. Alternatively, they may not feel confident enough in the distributor to purchase from them. Instead, they may prefer to go to a different one who is going to be more productive and helpful.

When you join an MLM company, make a clear and honest effort to know everything that you can about the business, the industry, and any trends that may be rising in it. Knowing everything you can ensures that you can market yourself as an expert, and people feel confident in coming to you and asking you any questions they might have.

They Didn't Target Their Niche Effectively

When people market but are not clear and specific in who they are marketing to, no one ends up listening. Marketing heavily relies on people relating to you and your message. However, when people are not specific in their message, they end up sharing things that are not really that relatable. People want to feel like they can personally relate on a deep level when they are reading things. This is how they stay interested. This is also how they know that the product or service is specifically meant for them.

When you are marketing to people, refrain from being too vague in your marketing. It can be tempting to try and market to an entire industry, but this is not effective. You will end up washing yourself out and not being recognized as someone who actually knows what they are doing. Instead, stay focused and market specifically. You will get way more engagement, and you will grow far faster.

They Tried to Make Things Too Complicated

People who are not really sure of what it takes to run a business have a tendency to overcomplicate things. One of the reasons that they join an MLM business is because everything is clearly set out for them, and it is easy for them to identify exactly what needs to be done. However, once they begin, they start trying to do things in a way that makes it far too complicated. As a result, they struggle to find new prospects and convert them because they are trying to do way more than they actually need to.

Instead of trying to overcomplicate things, focus on making things as simple as possible—the easier, the better. Avoid letting your boredom or impatience get the best of you, as this can quickly result in you trying to do more to fill the time. All that will end up happening is you fill your time with activities that kill your business. Don't do that.

They Got Impatient

MLM success stories are filled with people who got rich, but very few people actually take the time to realize what it took to get there or how long. As a result, people have this illusion that joining an MLM company means that they are going to get rich quick and that it will be easy. This is not the case. As with any other industry, building a strong MLM company requires you to take your time and be patient. The stronger of a foundation you build, the stronger of a company you are going to have. However, if you are not willing to put in that time, which most people aren't, it can result in quitting before you ever actually create any success.

Instead of getting into an MLM business assuming that you are going to be wildly successful and then growing impatient and quitting before you even get there, slow down. Be realistic about what you want and what it is going to take for you to get there. Find a way that you can keep yourself busy during those times when you feel bored or impatient, and stay focused on what the end result is going to be. This will keep you from quitting before you ever have the chance to become successful.

They Chose to Blame Others for Their Mistakes or Failures

When people get into an MLM company, and they do not start seeing the results they want within a specific period of time, it is not uncommon to see people starting to blame those around them—that, or they will begin to blame circumstances. It happens all the time: a person joins an MLM thinking it will be great and then proceeds to blame the economy, the industry, their team, or clients for not helping them become successful. So, thinking that they have done their best and that there was nothing else they could have possibly done, they quit and move on.

This is a huge mistake. First off, if you ever fail in any business, you have to be willing to shoulder the responsibility. In the end, it comes down to you not taking the time to learn what goes into making the business a success and then committing to the business until success happens for you. It has nothing to do with anything other than you. If you choose a company that's unable to help you generate success, that is because you haven't done your research. If prospects do not convert to clients, that is because you've never stopped to learn how to help them convert. If you have not generated the income you want, it is because you haven't done what you need to in order to generate that income.

This can sound harsh, but being willing to shoulder the responsibility is actually empowering. When you realize that the only person who is capable of helping you fail or succeed is you, then you realize that all of the power is in your hands. As a result, there is absolutely no reason why you cannot make your business work and generate the level of income that you desire.

They Never Actually Wanted to Succeed

Lastly, a big reason that people fail in their businesses is that they never actually wanted to succeed. This may sound crazy when you think about it, but truthfully, not everyone goes into their business with a strong desire to succeed. Some go in without any intention of doing anything with the opportunity. Some simply want the goodies that come in the kit or the potential for the opportunity to be there if they decide they want to. And some will go into it because they feel like they are being pressured. Not everyone joins an MLM company because they want to succeed or because they believe they can.

The only way to overcome this is to make sure that you go in with a strong intention and clear reason to your actions. If you go into your business and do not stay focused and dedicated to your commitment, then you may not have actually been that devoted to succeeding in the first place. The only way you can fix that is to look inside and figure out what have made you lose interest.

Conclusion

Congratulations on finishing *Insanely Effective Network and Multi-Level Marketing for Introverts on Social Media*!

The very fact that you have read the entire book proves that you are clearly dedicated to making your network marketing business a success. I hope that in reading this book, you felt that you were able to find all of the resources that you needed in order to truly generate the success that you desire.

Building a network marketing business and earning an income is a powerful way of taking your earnings into your own hands and living the kind of life that you want to live. When you do this, you give yourself an unlimited earning potential and the ability to live any lifestyle that you desire. Whether you want to live cozily in your home or travel the world, you can do anything you want when you put in the effort and grow your business effectively.

It is important that you realize that as great as this book is, there is always more you need to learn. Staying dedicated to learning and focusing on what more you can do to generate success are great ways to continue growing and establishing a stronger business for yourself. The more you devote to learning about what marketing strategies exist and how you can make the most of them, the better chance at success you are going to have.

Marketing is constantly changing, and new strategies are always being added. Taking the time to learn about what these strategies are, how they work, and how you can incorporate them into an attraction marketing method is a great way to continue growing your business. If you want to continue growing, you have to stay relevant.

The next thing you should do after reading this book is start laying a strong foundation for your business. Use the steps that I provided you to find the best company for you to join. Then, go ahead and get started with that company. Once you have, you can begin applying the marketing tools that I taught you so that you can begin getting the word out there. If you can, it would be beneficial for you to find a few blogs or podcasters who are in the MLM industry as well. That way, you can follow them and listen to their podcasts or read their posts to gain more inspiration. Make sure that you follow people who are actually generating great results so that you do not begin picking up on and practicing negative or difficult marketing strategies. Remember: your reputation is important, and a few bad marketing moves can really mess it up.

As you continue growing, always look for opportunities to learn more and do better. Even though you are marketing yourself as the expert, every true expert knows that there is never a cap on how much you can learn. Putting in the effort to constantly learn and grow ensures that you will stay an expert and that people will continue coming to you over anyone else when it comes to the services or products that you offer.

In addition to focusing on your growth in your industry, you also need to focus on your growth as a leader. The more people that are recruited under you, the more you are going to need to step up and lead your team effectively. Take the time to learn how to be an effective leader so that people feel confident being led by you and that they come to you instead of any other potential leaders.

Lastly, if you enjoyed this book, please take the time to honestly rate it on Amazon Kindle. Your feedback would be greatly appreciated.

Thank you, and good luck!

Book Description

Insanely Effective Network and Multi-Level Marketing for Introverts on Social Media is a powerful guide that is going to help you get started in network marketing even if you are an introvert.

Network Marketing and Multi-Level Marketing (MLM) companies are an incredible opportunity for virtually anyone to get started with. These companies offer a great source of income that can help you with anything from paying some of your monthly bills to completely replacing your traditional salary.

When done properly, network marketing is easily one of the best business decisions you can possibly make. Since most of the business is already laid out for you, you truly only need to master three things: marketing, leading, and building relationships. When you can master these three things, you can easily generate the success that you desire from a network marketing company. I am going to show you exactly how you can do that.

Purchase your copy of *Insanely Effective Network and Multi-Level Marketing for Introverts on Social Media* today to discover how you can build your own successful network marketing empire–even as an introvert–and begin claiming the life that you desire in no time at all. This book is filled with proven and effective growth strategies that you can guarantee will take you to the top!